# *Balance Sheet*

*From Confusion to Comfort in Under 30 Pages*

*By Axel Tracy*

Text Copyright © 2013 Bidi Capital Pty Ltd
All rights reserved.

**Cover Design:** Natural Selection Web Design LLC

## Disclaimer

The material in this publication (the "book") and the information accessed through it is of a general nature only and does not contain investment recommendations or professional advice. The information is not to be relied upon as being accurate, complete or up to date. Axel Tracy (the "author") recommends that, before acting or not acting upon information contained or referred to in this book, readers should seek independent professional advice that takes into account their financial situation, investment objectives, particular needs and/or other personal circumstances. The information contained in this book is not to be used for any purpose other than educational purposes and it is not to be construed as an indication or prediction of future results from any investment. Axel Tracy does not offer financial, business or academic advice. To the maximum extent permitted by law, the author and publisher disclaim all responsibility and liability to any person, arising from directly or indirectly from any person taking or not taking action based upon the information in this publication.

***For Georgina:*** *Thanks for helping me realise that, if all this doesn't work out, I still have a place somewhere.*

***For Jacqui & Jenny:*** *Thanks for showing me a world I never knew existed.*

# Table of Contents

About the Author ................................................................... 5
About accofina.com ............................................................. 6
Introduction .......................................................................... 7
Example Balance Sheet ........................................................ 9
What the Balance Sheet Shows…in under 2 Pages ............. 13
The Balance Sheet Equality ................................................ 17
Current & Non-Current Definitions ................................... 19
Assets ................................................................................... 20
    Current Assets ................................................................. 23
    Non-Current Assets ......................................................... 25
Liabilities ............................................................................. 32
    Current Liabilities ........................................................... 35
    Non-Current Liabilities .................................................. 38
Equity .................................................................................. 41
Links between the Balance Sheet and the Income Statement (the Profit & Loss Statement) ............................................ 45
Conclusion ........................................................................... 47
Extras ................................................................................... 48
    Book Excerpt ................................................................... 48
    Free accofina.com Books ................................................ 53
    Free accofina.com Spreadsheets .................................... 53
    More Books and Other accofina Products .................... 55
    Author Contact Details and Review Requests ............... 57

# About the Author

Axel Tracy is an accounting and business student at the University of Technology, Sydney. He has a passion for his studies and has been accepted into the invitation-only Golden Key International Honours Society in recognition of having a GPA that placed him in the top bracket of students at his university.

He was until recently also employed by the University of Technology, Sydney, to run PASS sessions in the subject of Accounting Standards and Regulations; an undergraduate accounting subject that trains students to become familiar with Australia's implementation of International Financial Reporting Standards and the current Australian accounting standard regime.

Since April, 2011, he has been the Founder & Director of Bidi Capital Pty Ltd, a holding company with two internet businesses revolving around accounting & finance (accofina.com & RatioAnalysis.net). Bidi Capital has had average quarterly revenue growth of 194% over the past two years.

Axel lives in inner city Sydney, Australia.

You can find Axel's Amazon Author Page at:
**amazon.com/author/axeltracy**

# About accofina.com

**accofina.com** launched in August, 2013, and is a hub for accounting & finance knowledge and technology.

On the website you will find Books, Apps, Online Courses & Tutorials, MS Excel Spreadsheets and other Online Calculators all customized to assist putting academic accounting & finance knowledge, through technology, in the hands of businesspeople, investors and students.

accofina.com is part of Bidi Capital Pty Ltd, which is a company founded, directed and owned by this book's author, Axel Tracy.

# Introduction

Whether you are running a business or analysing an investment, you will no doubt be provided with the financial statements of the business. These statements can be daunting if you are unsure about how to read them, yet it is imperative to have some accounting knowledge if you want to know the true state of a business. The financial statements, in short, give you a condensed glance into the financial success of any business.

While country-specific regulation dictates which financial statements must be prepared by an entity, the three key financial statements are:

1) The Income Statement (The Profit & Loss Statement)
2) The Balance Sheet (The Statement of Financial Position)
3) The Cash Flow Statement

This book will cover the basics of (2) The Balance Sheet, and will be part of a series of all three of these statements.

This book is not aimed at accountants or financial advisors, it is aimed at those who are provided with financial statements yet do not have an accounting background. Warren Buffett has said that accounting is the "language of business" so this book should hopefully teach you a few key 'phrases' that will allow you to converse about, and navigate around, the balance sheet. Will you become an expert from this book alone? No, but the beauty of the key financial statements is that a basic level of knowledge will allow you to make leaps and bounds when it comes to extracting value from the statements; in this case, the balance sheet.

Hopefully you should be able to tear through this read in one or two sittings, and you'll be prepped to make better business and investment decisions the next time someone hands you a balance sheet.

The structure of this book is pretty straightforward. Important concepts behind the balance sheet are covered along with outlines and descriptions of its components. Immediately after this introduction you will find an example balance sheet, and you can refer to this example as you progress through the chapters.

I am educated in accounting…and not educated in writing! I write because I like to help people learn accounting concepts…and I am passionate about accounting! I mention this because while I'd love to be a best-selling author, I know I will never become a best-writing author. The best I can hope for is that I become a better writer through each book being published over time. You can help me achieve these two goals:

If you want to help me become a better writer, please email me at **axel@accofina.com** and give me your suggestions for improvement.

If you want to help me become a best-selling author, please leave a positive review for this book (and maybe a comment on how it helped you) on Amazon.com.

So let's get into it!

Take a look at the Balance Sheet on the next page, look at its components and headings and then dive into the rest of this eBook. Best wishes!

# Example Balance Sheet

**Amazon.com Inc. (NASDAQ: AMZN)**

**Balance Sheet for 31st December, 2012**

Extracted from Google Finance (**https://www.google.com/finance**), a great free site for company analysis.

(In Millions of USD)

*Assets*

**Current Assets:**

| | |
|---|---|
| Cash & Equivalents | $8,084 |
| Short-Term Investments | $3,364 |
| Accounts Receivable – Net | $3,364 |
| Inventory | $6,031 |
| Prepaid Expenses | $0 |
| Other Current Assets | $453 |
| **Total Current Assets** | **$21,296** |

**Non-Current Assets:**

| | |
|---|---|
| Property, Plant & Equipment (PPE) – Cost | $9,582 |
| Accumulated Depreciation (PPE) | ($2,522) |
| Goodwill – Net | $2,552 |
| Intangibles | $725 |
| Long Term Investments | $0 |
| Other Non-Current Assets | $922 |
| **Total Non-Current Assets** | **$11,259** |

| | |
|---|---|
| *Total Assets* | $32,555 |

## *Liabilities*

**Current Liabilities:**

| | |
|---|---|
| Accounts Payable | $13,318 |
| Accrued Expenses | $5,684 |
| Notes Payable/Short Term Debt | $0 |
| Current portion of Long Term Debt/Capital Leases | $0 |
| Other Current Liabilities | $0 |
| **Total Current Liabilities** | **$19,002** |

**Non-Current Liabilities:**

| | |
|---|---|
| Long Term Debt | $3,084 |
| Capital/Finance Lease Obligations | $746 |
| Deferred Income Tax Liabilities | $0 |
| Other Liabilities | $1,531 |
| **Total Non-Current Liabilities** | **$5,361** |

*Total Liabilities* — $24,363

## *Equity*

| | |
|---|---|
| Common Stock – Total | $5 |
| Additional Paid in Capital | $8,347 |
| Retained Earnings | $1,916 |
| Treasury Stock – Common | ($1837) |
| Other Equity | ($239) |

*Total Equity* — *$8,192*

*Total Liabilities & Equity* — $32,555

Note: While I tried to make this balance sheet as practical as possible, there is no global standard on how you set out a balance sheet. Sure, assets, liabilities & equity are always there, but different countries include different specifics. This may include account names (the balance sheet line items) and of course currencies.

What's more is that as the size and complexity of a business grows, so does the complexity of the balance sheet. This book is published as part of a small business, and if you looked at my company's balance sheet you would see it is far simpler and has less accounts than a behemoth like Amazon Inc. So, if you have a balance sheet for your business and things don't match up exactly to what's above or what's on Google Finance, then don't stress, just keep in mind that the following sections should appear in all balance sheets:

- Assets
  - Current Assets
  - Non-Current Assets
- Liabilities
  - Current Liabilities
  - Non-Current Liabilities
- Equity
  - Capital
  - Retained Earnings
  - Current Earnings (if the balance sheet is prepared during the financial year)

Also, just before we jump ahead, take a look at the equality between assets and then liabilities plus equity: these MUST always balance. Assets must be equal to the sum of liabilities and equity. This is just part of double-entry accounting (a topic outside the scope of this book). But another way to look at it is: your assets must always be financed by debt (liabilities) and/or equity. In other words, you can't pay for something in the business unless you get the money from somewhere, such as a bank, investors or the business earnings (current and retained earnings).

Finally, I have tried to take what's on Google Finance and

reproduce it above for the novice reader. So if you take a look online yourself, you will see it's not an exact replica. Again, don't stress, get a hold of the basics and you will eventually be able to analyse any balance sheet out there. If you do want to look at the Google Finance balance sheet, follow these steps:

1) Go to **www.google.com/finance**
2) In the "Search Finance" box, type: Amazon.com and choose Amazon.com, Inc. from the search drop-down
3) Under the Company Menu (left-hand side) choose "Financials"
4) Click Balance Sheet
5) Click Annual Data
6) You will now find the above balance sheet where "As of 2012-12-31" lies.

# What the Balance Sheet Shows…in under 2 Pages

So why do we have a balance sheet in the first place? Why are you reading this book?

Here's the super-short answer:

A balance sheet shows (denominated in currency) what a business:
1) Owns/Controls (Assets)
2) Owes/Obligated to do (Liabilities)
3) And what's left when you subtracted [2] from [1]: What is left for the owners' of the business (Equity)

That's really all there is to it!

If you wanted to produce a balance sheet for a company like Amazon.com then that would take years of study and practice, and many others (just as skilled as you) to help you…but you can't hide the fact that the end result of any balance sheet is just in the numbered list above.

So what use is this information?

Well, the first word of caution is that while the Balance Sheet is vital for company analysis, it is not a stand-alone statement. You generally need to look at the other financial statements (e.g. Income Statement and Statement of Cash Flows) to get the true picture of what is going on behind the numbers.

But leaving that word of caution aside, there is still lots you can understand from a balance sheet.

First, look at the assets (what the company owns). Assets have a complicated definition in the financial accounting handbook but essentially assets are what generate future income of the business. A company purchases, or holds, assets in the hope that they will produce more income than they cost to buy or hold. Simple. Look at "Inventory" (Current Assets) in the example Balance Sheet; this account represents goods that Amazon.com has purchased in the hope that it can later re-sell them at a higher price. Or "Property, Plant & Equipment" (Non-Current Assets), this account represents the property, plant & equipment (go figure!) that Amazon.com has purchased that will hopefully help their business run smoothly (such as a warehouse and logistics machinery), which will in turn hopefully lead it to sell more books like this one.

Next, look at the liabilities (what the company owes). Again, there is a complicated definition for liabilities in the handbook, but generally what it refers to are the obligations that lead to outflows of currency at later date(s) to satisfy these same obligations. In short, you can think of them as simply the debts of the business.

These debts can represent how you funded the assets on the other side of the balance sheet (note: you can also fund them through equity). For instance, you took on a bank loan of $100,000 (a liability) to purchase a retail shop for a business (an asset in the property, plant and equipment line item). And then this asset will hopefully lead to income in the future.

The final section is equity. Now I have talked about the financial accounting handbook definitions of the previous two components, but the definition of equity is rather abstract in that is based on a derivative of the previous two definitions (of assets & liabilities). The better way to look at equity is to think of it as what is left for the owners of the business if all the assets were liquidated and the liabilities paid off. Equity represents owner, or shareholder, funds that have been invested, or retained, in the business (although this is not the exact definition).

Similar to liabilities, equity can also be a source of funds to pay for assets. So rather than take out that bank loan to buy the retail shop, the business could sell stock/shares in the business for $100,000 and then buy the shop, or simply use the funds it has earned in business operations (as these 'Retained Earnings' are also equity).

Let's put it all together in a timeline:
(1) A business is incorporated and starts its life
(2) It raises money through taking on liabilities or issuing equity
(3) It uses this money to buy assets
(4) The assets generate income
(5) The income can pay for more assets or the cycle repeats from stage (2)

But outside of this timeline, never forget than any balance sheet simply shows a snapshot in time of what a business:
- "Owns" (assets)
- "Owes" (liabilities)
- "What is left for the owners of the business" (equity)

If you can remember this then you can start to paint a picture of the business.

For instance, you can tell how the management likes to finance the business (does it have higher liabilities or higher equity), you can look at line items and see how the assets are structured (e.g. does it have lots of cash or lots of fixed, non-current assets), whether the business is over-leveraged (are liabilities too high in relation to assets), etc.

These are just a few examples, just think about what the components of the balance sheet represent, spend time analyzing the overall figures and relationships and start to paint that picture of what is going on underneath all those raw numbers.

# The Balance Sheet Equality

I mentioned this briefly in the Example Amazon Balance Sheet Section, and also mentioned double-entry accounting. While not explaining double-entry accounting in full, I do want to talk about the Balance Sheet Equality.

The balance sheet equality is based on the "Accounting Equation".

Simply, the accounting equation is a rule that must hold. If it does not hold then that is an immediate signal that you have made a mistake in your accounting processes, your double-entry accounting.

Here is the equation:

**Assets = Liabilities + Equity**

Like I mentioned earlier, to finance an asset you must source those funds from liabilities or equity (or both). For example, when assets go up by, say, $10,000 then either you have taken on a liability and/or issued equity for the same amount of $10,000, and the accounting equation will hold. None of the components, assets, liabilities or equity can simply 'appear' (or disappear) without another component (or the same component, but a different account line item) being affected.

Try it out for yourself…have a look at Amazon's Balance Sheet and see if any of the items (or 'accounts' as they're properly called) could just 'appear'. When you realize they couldn't, try and see which corresponding account(s) could be affected by a change in the initial account you are looking at. For example, where did Cash & Cash Equivalents come from? It could be a loan (liability), from current earnings (equity), from issuing stock/shares (equity again) or maybe even from selling some property, plant and equipment or inventory (assets themselves), etc.

The accounting equation is at the heart of 'double-entry accounting'. This is the idea that not only does every transaction affect an account of assets, liabilities or equity, but also every transaction affects *at least two accounts* (hence double-entry) within these components. Without going into a lesson about 'debits' and 'credits' (the core theory behind recording transactions in the double-entry system), the fact that each transaction affects at least two accounts means that the accounting equation MUST always balance. It's not that YOU must make it balance, it's simply that if it doesn't balance then there has been a clerical error in recording a transaction within a double-entry system. For example, remember that $100,000 loan to buy the retail shop? Well, that would be Liabilities increasing by $100,000 (the loan) and Assets increasing by $100,000 (the retail shop)…and the equation holds. This example can be replicated (and the accounting equation will still hold) by every single transaction any possible business is making or ever could make. It is simply that comprehensive…a pretty powerful concept behind what is too often raw, not-understood numbers on a simple, 1-page balance sheet.

# Current & Non-Current Definitions

Okay, let's cover some jargon now that will bleed through the rest of this book...

In the balance sheet, both assets and liabilities are broken down into "Current" and "Non-Current". What does this mean? It is simply accountants' jargon defining time periods.

'Current' means the asset will be "realized" (used up or turned into cash) within the next 12-month period. A 'Non-Current" asset is just an asset that will be realized beyond the next 12-month period. Twelve months from the date of the balance sheet is the line in the sand, the barrier between current and non-current.

The flip side is true for liabilities. All liabilities that must be settled (paid back) within the next 12-months are considered 'Current' liabilities. Those that don't need to be settled for at least 12-months are considered 'Non-Current' liabilities.

# Assets

*"An asset is a resource controlled by the entity as a result of past events, and from which future economic benefits are expected to flow to the entity"*

- IASB Conceptual Framework: Chapter 4 The Framework; paragraph 4.4(a)

The definition above is the 'complicated' definition of an asset, which I mentioned earlier. The definition comes from the International Accounting Standards Board (IASB), a financial accounting standards (rules) organization that sets the standards for all nations who follow international accounting standards.

Breaking the jargon down, the definition is not too complicated. An asset is something that is "controlled" by a business (like a factory) due to a "past" transaction (buying the factory), which causes a flow to the business of "future economic benefits", i.e. income will be derived from using the asset in the future (the factory will produce goods in the future that will be sold for income).

Technically, anything that fits inside the above definition could be called an asset. And these are what sit at the top of the balance sheet.

The key idea is that an asset is acquired and/or held by a business in order to generate, or access, cash from it in the future.

Generally, the convention is that assets are listed in order of liquidity down the balance sheet. That means that the most liquid assets (e.g. cash) sit at the top of the list of assets and the least liquid (perhaps an oil transport tanker) sit at the bottom. The term "liquidity" simply refers to the ability to turn the asset into cash. If the asset is considered highly liquid, then it is easy to convert into cash, if it considered highly illiquid, then it is hard to convert into cash.

Taking on board these key ideas, have a look at the Amazon Inc. balance sheet. What can you deduce from the assets listed in this financial statement? Are the highest asset values located near the top, implying lots of liquid assets? What does each asset value tell you about the Amazon business model, e.g. does it use high levels of equipment fixed assets, or possibly have high levels of accounts receivable?

I cannot stress enough the concept of asking yourself, when you look at the balance sheet, "what does this tell me?" If you spend enough time analyzing the accounts, you can start to draw inferences about the business. For example, I just mentioned testing whether the accounts receivable is high, you could spend time comparing the accounts receivable balance over time (over multiple balance sheets) and test if this asset figure is rising or falling. A fall may mean that the business is improving its collections operations, or maybe that it is tightening its credit policy. When you draw one conclusion, you can often check its validity by looking at other sections of the financial statements. For example, if the business was tightening its credit policy, what has happened to sales revenue in the Income Statement? One could assume that a very tight credit policy might mean fewer sales as fewer clients would qualify for credit.

While this last paragraph is more about financial statement analysis rather than understanding balance sheets, I hope you can appreciate the idea that while this concise book can help you get your head around a balance sheet you can always learn more and get more value from all financial statements.

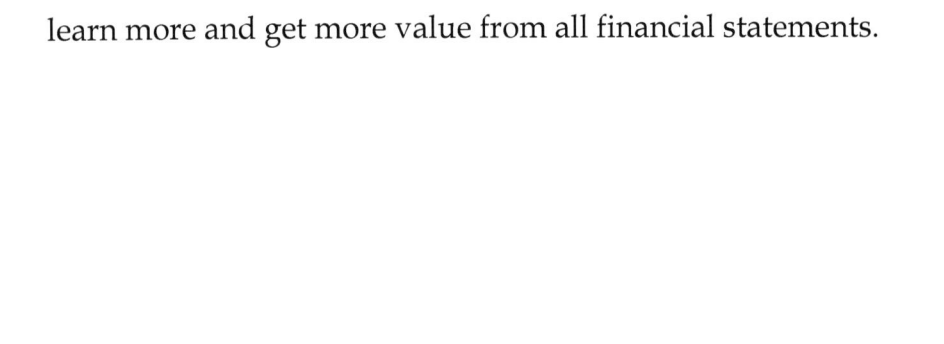

# Current Assets

Now that we've covered the definitions of 'current' and 'assets' we can take a little more time looking at specific current assets.

Remembering that the current assets are the most liquid since they are at the top of the balance sheet, you will soon realize that many current assets are, in fact, monetary in nature. That is, they are a claim to some sort of finances. Where the Property, Plant & Equipment (a non-current asset) value represents something like a factory in a city, many of the current assets specifically represent financial claims (like 'Cash' or 'Accounts Receivable').

Let's add a quick finance concept before moving onto analyzing current assets...

We mentioned that asset liquidity refers to assets ability to be converted to cash. You may ask why a business would give up liquid assets (which can pay the invoices that come in or pay dividends to owners) for less liquid assets (which may involve a lengthy process before using them to pay the invoices or dividends)? The answer lies in the general principle that a business (or even an individual) gives up liquidity in order to (hopefully) obtain a higher return from the asset. Look at Amazon Inc's top two current assets, 'Cash & Equivalents' and 'Short-Term Investments': now both are highly liquid (they both sit right at the top), but from their order you can see that cash is more liquid than short-term investments. Now that makes sense, you can simply go to your bank and make a withdrawal from Cash today, yet you may need a few days or few weeks to sell the Short-Term Investments and wait for the delayed settlement to realize their cash value. But look what also makes sense: do you expect a higher return from your checking account interest rate (Cash & Equivalents) or from your corporate bonds (Short-Term Investments)? While not only fitting into the 'Current Assets' section alone, this lesson is important to remember for the rest of this book and your own balance sheet analysis.

Now with this lesson under our belt, what can we learn from the current assets section of a balance sheet? One, of many, things we can draw is that we can test how 'secure' the business will be at maintaining its operations. As mentioned, you can generally only pay the business' bills with cash, and you only really ever go out of business if you can't pay your bills. So knowing this we can look at the structure of a business' current assets. If 'Inventory' is too high, it may mean that the entity can't sell is stock or maintain optimal stock levels in-store. If 'Accounts Receivable' is too high then it may mean that the entity can't collect its debts adequately. Yet, if the more liquid current assets are too high, then this may mean that the entity is forsaking a higher return on its assets for the sake of having lots of cash and short-term investments. Knowing what to look for, and how to interpret values, will take practice, but even within these past few pages you can begin to start telling the story of the business from what may have been an almost 'foreign' set of line items and values.

# Non-Current Assets

Next we are looking at non-current assets; these being the assets that are expected to last, or remain on the balance sheet (individually) for more than 12-months.

We spend quite a bit of time on non-current assets in comparison to other sections. The reason for this is two-fold.

First, there are some new accounting concepts and terminology introduced into this section of the balance sheet. It makes non-current assets not as quickly understandable as some of the other sections of the statement. Therefore we go into a few specific accounts inside non-current assets and try to explain the accounting and jargon behind them.

Secondly, more likely than not, the non-current assets are vital to the operation and success of the business. This is because very often the revenue-generation capabilities of a business are based on its ability to turn non-current assets into sales. Investments in non-current assets are what lead to future sales. As you read the sections below try imagining any business without an efficient set of non-current assets, generally there would be no business at all. All accounts of the balance sheet play their part and have a role in managing a business, but it is success (or lack of it) of investments in non-current assets that lead to the income-production success of a business. Refer back to the Current Asset section and our discussion on liquidity. We said that liquidity is often given up for a higher return on the assets. This implies the least liquid assets (the non-current assets) can earn the highest returns and may lead to the highest success for the business. Truly understanding this section of the balance sheet, and spending more time on it, leads to a better understanding of the revenue-generation profile of any business.

Firstly, let's look at Amazon's non-current assets. While a couple of accounts, i.e. Property, Plant & Equipment (PPE) and Long Term Investments are things we have already covered or are otherwise self explanatory, there are a few accounts in our example balance sheet that you will see in many other businesses and deserve special attention. These are Accumulated Depreciation, Intangibles & Goodwill.

*Accumulated Depreciation:*

When a non-current asset is purchased, such as an item of PPE, the cost of the asset goes straight on the balance sheet without appearing in the corresponding Profit & Loss Statement in the Expenses section. This is just a rule of accounting, but does this mean that a hypothetical $50,000 Forklift never appears as an expense for the business? The answer is 'No' and the 'Depreciation Expense' account gives the explanation. Without going too deep into some of the fundamental principles of accounting, specifically the 'matching principle', try to look at it like this:

If Amazon buys a $50,000 forklift in January, 2014, and that forklift is expected to carry orders from warehouse shelves to delivery trucks for *two full years*, then which Profit and Loss Statement structure would look more accurate (1) A full $50,000 PPE Expense in the January 2014 Profit and Loss Statement and therefore $0 PPE Expense for every profit and loss statement from there, or (2) considering the forklift will help generate revenue for *two full years* (and hence is an asset), we should have 24 separate monthly profit and loss statements (if we report monthly) and recognize a portion of the $50,000 as an expense in each of the separate 24 statements, i.e. $2,083.33 PPE Expense for each month over 24-months ($50,000/24 = $2,083.33). The answer is (2) because as accountants we better reflect the true state of the business if we 'match' the expenses against the revenue they generate, i.e. we 'match' the $50,000 Forklift expense against the 24-months of revenue it helps generate by delivering the orders for *two full years*.

If you are still with me at this point, then great, because you now probably understand the most common misconception that faces university accounting students. Now let's complete the circle:

In the example we just explained in the above paragraph, we actually don't recognize a $2,083.33 PPE Expense in each of the 24 monthly profit and loss statements. Instead we use a 'catch-all' account called Depreciation, so in each of those 24 statements we would have a $2,083.33 'Depreciation' Expense.

Okay, we're almost there. So, I have been talking a lot about depreciation 'expenses' and profit and loss statements…yet this is a book about balance sheets! Well, this is an example of where the two statements link. Because when every profit and loss statement is prepared and there is a depreciation expense, then this depreciation expense amount (an exact dollar figure) is transferred to the balance sheet and added to a running total of all depreciation to date for each separate depreciable non-current asset account. This running total is known as 'Accumulated Depreciation' and is known as a 'contra asset' account, meaning that the balance is negative and is subtracted from the particular non-current asset account on the balance sheet.

Taking all this on board, let's return to our forklift example:

Let's imagine it is now April, 2014, and we are looking at our March balance sheet and we have already completed January, February & March profit and loss statements. Our March balance sheet would have something like this:

**Non-Current Assets:**
PPE                                              $50,000
*(The original cost of the forklift)*
Accumulated Depreciation – PPE       ($6,250)
*(A negative balance that is the sum of $2,083.33 depreciation expenses in each of January, February & March)*
**Total Non-Current Assets**        **$43,750**
*(Cost minus Depreciation or $50,000 minus $6,250)*

With all of this wrapped up, hopefully you now know the concept of an Accumulated Depreciation account and why it has a negative balance. There is a little more to depreciation that what has been explained, but the key ideas outlined will always hold.

Note: We just talked about a link between the balance sheet and the income statement. If you are keen to also learn more about the income statement, check out *"Income Statement Basics: From Confusion to Comfort in Under 30 Pages"* **(http://accofina.com/books/income-statement-basics.html)**. This is the second title of this series written by Axel Tracy (this book's author)

The next 'tricky' account is Intangibles.

*Intangibles:*

Now, I just said this account was 'tricky', but if you can get around some accounting jargon then you should understand this account with knowledge we have already covered.

The International Accounting Standards Board (the 'rule' makers of the financial accounting profession) defines an Intangible as "an identifiable non-monetary asset without physical substance"…let's break this down:

First, it's an asset. Simple.

Next, it's an asset without physical substance. This is kind of like saying you can't 'touch' it. This includes things like legal rights (e.g. patents) and computer code (e.g. software). This is opposed to an asset with physical substance, like a crane or a truck.

It's non-monetary: this simply means it is not a type of asset that represents a financial claim. Cash and Accounts Receivable are both monetary assets; their values represent a specific claim to a specific amount of cash. Therefore, all these type of monetary assets can't be classified as intangibles, even though they may meet all other criteria.

Finally, it's "identifiable". This is accounting jargon that means the asset can be separated from the business and hypothetically sold individually. Using software as an example, your business could separate your MS Office software (it wouldn't destroy your business…you simply couldn't use MS Excel, MS Word, etc.) from the rest of your business and sell the software as an individual item (if you had the hypothetical legal right to do this). These qualities of your MS Office software makes this productivity package an 'identifiable' asset.

Pull all these explanations together and we know what an Intangible Asset is. Depending on the industry, they can often be a large and vital component of a businesses asset base. Think about software companies, how much of their value is made up of the intangible patents they own and the in-house software systems they use. The industry can also determine what type of intangibles a business has. As just explained, software companies have high levels of patents, casino companies may have high levels of gaming licenses, music companies have high levels of copyright assets, and so on.

Before we move on, do intangibles depreciate like some other non-current assets? The answer is 'sometimes' and 'not exactly'. It's 'sometimes' because some intangible have an indefinite life (and are not depreciated) and some intangibles do have a set useful life, like a patent lasting 20 years (and are depreciated). And it's 'not exactly' because intangibles don't actually depreciate, they "amortize". This is just more accounting terminology and effectively is identical to depreciation…except we have Amortization Expense and Accumulated Amortization, and not depreciation.

*Goodwill:*

The final account we are looking at is Goodwill.

Firstly, goodwill is a type of intangible asset but has it's own account.

Next, goodwill has two meanings, yet only one will ever apply to the balance sheet. 'Goodwill' can often refer to the positive feeling, mood or attitude towards a business: a business with great customer service has goodwill, a business with strong brand loyalty has goodwill, etc. But this type of *internally generated* goodwill is NEVER shown on the balance sheet.

The type of Goodwill in Amazon's balance sheet (and all other balance sheets) is *purchased* goodwill. What is 'purchased' goodwill? You probably know that many companies make acquisitions of other business, e.g. Google buying YouTube, Bank of America buying Merrill Lynch, etc. Purchased goodwill is a result of the accounting of these corporate transactions.

Essentially, when a business buys another business it is paying $x for the $y value of the Equity or Net Assets (value of assets minus liabilities) of the other business. Generally, to encourage the shareholders of the business being taken over to sell their stock to the acquiring company a premium must be paid. A good premium so the takeover offer seems attractive. This premium is why $x is generally higher than $y. And the difference ($z) between $x and $y is the purchased goodwill…and $z appears on the balance sheet as goodwill!

Let's use a quick example and remove the alphabet notation (note: this is a stylized example and not a representation of what really happened): Google wants to buy YouTube. YouTube has $100m of Net Assets (Assets minus Liabilities), but Google really wants the owners of YouTube to sell their stock to Google so they can take control. Therefore Google offers $1b to buy YouTube, a premium of $900m ($1b minus $100m). The Goodwill on Google's next balance sheet (post the YouTube acquisition) is $900m.

# Liabilities

*"A liability is a present obligation of the entity arising from past events, the settlement of which is expected to result in an outflow from the entity of resources embodying economic benefits."*

- IASB Conceptual Framework: Chapter 4 The Framework; paragraph 4.4(b)

Once again the definition provided by the IASB is rather convoluted. But before we write it off, have a look at it again and then go back to the IASB definition of assets. You will see that they are almost a mirror image of each other. Rather than being a "resource controlled" it is a "present obligation" and rather than "economic benefits...flow to the entity" it is "outflow from the entity of...economic benefits". So when an asset is something you have power over that creates inflows of cash, a liabilities is something you don't have power over (it's an obligation) that creates outflows of cash.

Again like assets, there are three key components of the definition. First it is a "present obligation", not a past or future obligation it is something you owe now (like the current electricity invoice). It is based on "past events", that is you will never find a liability on a balance sheet for an event that will happen in the future (you used the electricity last month to receive the current electricity invoice) and will result in an "outflow...of resources", meaning you will settle the liability by handing over a resource (generally cash, like when you pay the electricity bill).

But still, yes, the definition is complex, detailed and a little mind-bending. If you want to strip out all the detail and jargon, a liability is a 'debt', something you owe. Technically, anything that fits the formal IASB definition of a liability should be on the balance sheet and this definition is a bit broader than simply saying 'debts'.

From here on in you will start to see the same knowledge repeating itself, just maybe with a little twist or flip. The next concept to repeat itself is the accounts being sorted based on their liquidity. When assets were listed top to bottom based on liquidity, liabilities are ordered on the balance sheet from top to bottom based on when they have to be settled. The sooner the liability has to be settled, the higher up the order it is in the liabilities section.

Once again, liabilities are broken down into current and non-current categories and also once again, even with only the knowledge covered already, we can start to paint the picture behind the numbers. Look at Amazon's liabilities, look at the current and non-current breakdown, look at which liabilities are the highest and when the have to be settled. What is this picture telling us about Amazon?

Still not grasping it 100%? Think about it like this, why does a company go out of business (if not voluntarily wound-up or acquired by another company)? Basically the answer to this question is always because it can't pay it's debts and it or its creditors put it in bankruptcy or liquidation. Wait! What's another name for debts? Liabilities. And how do we pay/settle liabilities? Cash (generally). And cash is an asset. And how do we get cash? By getting a return from our current and non-current assets.

See how it's all starting to fit together. An analysis of a company's liabilities is often an analysis of business risk. So knowing what you know now, and what was explained in this section, take another look at Amazon's balance sheet and its liabilities and try to begin to tell a story about Amazon's liabilities and possible risk. Starting to see the beauty of a 1-page balance sheet, yet?

# Current Liabilities

Current liabilities on the balance sheet are those due within 12 months. This can immediately allow a quick check of the solvency status of any business. How? Simply look at the level of current liabilities and check against the level of current assets (what will pay these liabilities). Apart from a few large businesses with very high inventory turnover, this quick check is one the simplest applications of balance sheet analysis. When you build your confidence in handling financial statements and move onto ratio analysis, this quick check of measuring current assets and current liabilities is known as the 'current ratio' and is often used to test a business' ability to maintain normal operations without resorting to selling non-current assets or raising capital.

Apart from quick liquidity tests, the current liabilities can also give a sense of the structure of the long-term debt financing of a business. If you look at Amazon's balance sheet you'll see an account named 'Current portion of Long Term Debt/Capital Leases'. What this account represents is a transfer of long-term debt, which sits in non-current liabilities, to the current liabilities section, as this portion of this debt will be due in the coming year. Knowing this you can see how the long-term debt is structured: is the current portion remaining constant over time, meaning even and predictable payments going forward. Or is the current portion more lumpy, meaning that you will need to keep an eye on when a large 'chunk' of long term debt becomes due.

At the very top of current liabilities is Accounts Payable. This account is used for the operating expenses which are made on short term credit, for example it's kind of like that electricity invoice being sent out at the end of the month but you are given 30 days to pay it. All the operating expenses with any type of credit terms fall into accounts payable. Again, testing near term solvency and liquidity risk is the best application of analyzing accounts payable.

Leaving the most complicated till last, Accrued Expenses represents a function of accounting practice. One of the foundations of the study of accounting is the concept of 'accrual accounting'. In short, this means we recognize transactions 'as they occur' as opposed to only 'when cash payments are made'.

Putting it in an example: if your business pays $6,000 rent on a quarterly basis (i.e. you transfer $6,000 cash to your landlord in January, April, July & October) but you prepare financial statements on a monthly basis (i.e. every month January through December), then when should you have "Rent Expense" on your Profit & Loss statement? Should it be $6,000 each in January, April, July & October? Using 'accrual accounting' (and think back to the earlier depreciation explanation) we should recognize "Rent Expense" every time we prepare financial statements, after all, we have used the rental property every day of the year and not just in January, April, etc. Therefore, since we prepare financial statements monthly (January through December) we should recognize $2,000 ($6,000 / 3) "Rent Expense" in every month January through December. But in Feb & March, and every month where we don't receive a rent bill/invoice, where do we show the amount owing from the 'accrued' rent expense? We don't hand over cash in these months so our current asset Cash doesn't go down, and we don't have a bill yet in these months so we can't put the $2,000 in Accounts Payable. The answer lies in the Accrued Expenses account (still a liability account). In February we put $2,000 in Accrued Expenses, in March we put another $2,000 there and have a balance of $4,000 and then in April (when we actually get the bill or hand over cash) we show another $2,000 rent expense in our Profit & Loss Statement but we clear Accrued Expenses back to $0 and transfer the full $6,000 to accounts payable (if we have credit terms) or take the full $6,000 from the cash account (if we paid immediately as we don't have credit terms).

# Non-Current Liabilities

Next up we have non-current liabilities, and to be honest we are not going to spend as much time covering this section (in comparison to non-current assets). The reason for this is that, firstly, non-current liabilities are generally made of long-term debt and that concept should be self-explanatory, and secondly, a couple of the accounts within non-current liabilities are a little beyond the scope of this book; in fact you will find many early accounting graduates would struggle to adequately explain them to a novice who did not have formal university accounting training.

Let's cover the simple stuff:

Long-Term Debt is simply the loans that are due beyond 12-months. The dollar value given is simply what is left to be repaid, the loan principal in addition to accumulated interest. The major take-away from these figures are leverage analysis and, once again, risk analysis.

Leverage is term given to how much of a business is debt financed. It's termed leverage because it 'levers' the upside or downside. In other words, by increasing the capital base with a loan you can magnify your gains or magnify your losses depending on how successful your strategy and implementation is. So when you look at the Long-Term Debt figures, you can assess how aggressive a management is: have they been highly 'leveraging' their business, and if so, do they have the right strategy and implementation? Or is this increased debt putting the company at risk? Which leads into risk analysis. We have covered this a number of times already, but liabilities are a source of risk, so looking at Long-Term

Debt values allows us to measure the level of risk in the capital structure of the business.

The account Other Liabilities is simply a catchall for all more miscellaneous liabilities. And if we remember our formal IASB definition of liabilities, we can conclude that ANYTHING that fits that definition of liabilities has to be on the balance sheet. This can be pretty widely encompassing, so there needs to be some sort of catchall account.

Now to the stuff that requires deep training…so much so that we are going to brush over it with only a few pointers in this 'basics' book:

Firstly, the account "Capital/Finance Lease Obligations". In years past, accountants and large corporations devised an accounting 'trick' that could result in lower expenses, fewer liabilities & stronger accounting ratios and as a result improve their financial performance and borrowing capacity. This trick was to not borrow funds and then purchase large non-current assets but instead they leased them without borrowing any funds. The accounting behind this trick is too complicated for this book but when this practice became too widespread the financial accounting rule-setters like the IASB and other national equivalents (in the United States it is the FASB, the Financial Accounting Standards Board) responded by effectively outlawing this trick and forcing lease transactions that were substitutes for a 'borrow and purchase' transaction to be classified and accounted for very similarly to Long-Term Debt. In conclusion, what you need to know as a non-accountant is that the account "Capital/Finance Lease Obligations" is effectively identical to Long-Term Debt account, so you should aggregate these totals to find the true figure for non-current debts outstanding.

Finally, there is "Deferred Income Tax Liabilities". This account is there because reporting entities must use 'tax effect' accounting. Tax effect accounting as a concept is very difficult to get your head around, does not apply to all businesses, is the product of detailed and complicated (but hopefully more 'accurate') accounting theory and is often hotly-debated by accounting academics as to whether these 'liabilities' genuinely fit the definition of a liability. Thankfully, the figures for Deferred Income Tax Liabilities should be rather small and generally insignificant. For any novice, best to just acknowledge the figure and move on. For the record, there is also the possibility of having 'deferred income tax assets'.

# Equity

*"Equity is the residual interest in the assets of the entity after deducting all its liabilities."*

- IASB Conceptual Framework: Chapter 4 The Framework; paragraph 4.4(c)

You'll see from this IASB definition that equity doesn't have its own definition but one that is a derivative based on the of both the asset and liability definitions.

The key idea about equity is that it's the owners' interest in the business. From all operations to date, equity is the financial value that owners can call theirs. The company owns the assets, the shareholders own the company and if all liabilities are paid off, using the assets (remembering that liabilities are 'outsiders' claims on the assets), then what is remaining belongs to the owners.

Equity can have a number of names, from 'owners equity' or 'owners capital' (generally both used when it's a small business) to 'shareholder equity' (or 'stockholder equity', depending on your location) when the business is a company with shareholders. Whatever you call it, just remember the above definition and the "residual interest" belongs to owners of the business.

If you look at the Equity section of Amazon's Balance Sheet you will find a number of different accounts listed. The reality is there are a vast number of account possibilities when it comes to Equity and unless you are a professional analyst or advanced accountant the truth is there are only a few you

NEED to know about. We'll cover this now:

First, I want to combine two accounts for (a) simplicity, and (b) they may already be combined, depending on the country where you reside. These accounts are 'Common Stock' and 'Additional Paid in Capital'. These accounts represent what shareholders have contributed in funds to the business when there have been equity capital raisings. So if a company doesn't want to get its money from debt finance it can turn to its shareholders to put in more cash in exchange for shares or stock in the business; they can contribute funds in return for partial ownership of the business. For example, if Amazon sells 10,000 shares at $10 each, then it should add $100,000 (10,000 x $10) to the total of this account.

The next important equity account is one that doesn't even appear in Amazon's balance sheet at year-end, or any balance sheet at year-end. This account is 'Current Earnings'. Current Earnings appears throughout the financial year and is the current years profit (or loss) at that point in time. So if the business' financial year runs from January till December and profits at the end of April are $5,000, then the equity account 'Current Earnings' in the balance sheet will show a figure of $5,000.

We are now addressing the account 'Retained Earnings' and we will also explain why Amazon doesn't have a current earnings account in the example balance sheet I've given you. Retained Earnings (or Deficit) are the accumulated retained profits (or losses) of the business since its inception. A profit in year 1 of $400 plus a profit of $300 in year 2 would lead to a retained earnings balance of $700 after both years. If you think about it, the literal translation of 'retained earnings' is kind of self-explanatory; it's the profit (earnings) since inception that has been kept (retained) in the business.

So why doesn't Amazon have a Current Earnings account?

Well, depending on how the accounts are exactly prepared (I will use the simplest explanation), the current earnings balance (at year end when the final accounts are prepared) is closed off to retained earnings. That is, the current earnings balance is transferred to retained earnings; current earnings goes back to zero (because it's a new year with zero earnings for that year at that stage) and retained earnings is increased by the balance of current earnings (since now last years current earnings are effectively this years retained earnings). I just mentioned, "how the accounts are exactly prepared", I used this qualification because, according to Google Finance, Amazon never has a current earnings account, even in the quarterly reports. This could mean that Amazon (or Google Finance for simplicity) transfers current earnings to retained earnings every reporting period. However, this point is rather arbitrary, whichever way the balance sheet is presented to you, just know how what retained earnings is, and how any possible current earnings account is linked.

Before we leave the retained earnings account it's important to talk about dividends paid and where they fit into equity. While not on the Amazon balance sheet, all dividends a business makes are taken from the equity section. If you think about it, dividends are paid to shareholders so logically their recognition should also be from shareholders equity. Now, the exact accounting process can be done a few ways, but the key idea to remember is that all dividend amounts eventually come from retained earnings. Remember, retained earnings are profits kept in the business and dividends are paid out of profits, so effectively they are profits (earnings) NOT kept (not retained) in the business.

Before we leave equity, I'll just mention the 'Treasury Stock' account that Amazon has (as well as many other businesses). This accounts represents the value of shares, or stock, the company has purchased in its own business. If Amazon (as a corporation) purchases Amazon stock, the value of these

43

purchases is placed in Treasury Stock. Companies often do this to immediately raise the value of their own shares or to return funds to stockholders without paying dividends (by buying their stock back from them possibly at a good price). In regards to immediately raising the value of the shares, if Amazon purchases its own shares it takes them off the market and reduces the supply of Amazon shares. All other things being equal, a reduced supply (and constant demand) will push up the price of the remaining Amazon shares.

# Links between the Balance Sheet and the Income Statement (the Profit & Loss Statement)

The balance sheet and income statement are two of the three main financial statements (along with the cash flow statement), yet it is the balance sheet and income statement that are intricately linked. One reason behind this is the accounting concept of 'double-entry' accounting; a centuries old accounting practice where each business transaction affects at least two accounts. While double-entry accounting is the topic of another book, the two statements links may seem more logical if we look at one, simple example.

If Amazon sells a Kindle Book for $9.99 then logically 'sales revenue' (an income statement account) would increase by $9.99 but also their 'cash' balance (a balance sheet account) would also increase by $9.99. This simple illustration is just one of many examples of how accounts from one statement are linked to accounts in the other statement.

So, rather than detailing every possible example and eventuality, just remember that if you really want to develop your financial statement analysis skills then don't just stop with understanding the balance sheet. While I personally believe the cash flow statement is far underappreciated, overlooked and misunderstood, I still have to advise that, on your accounting knowledge journey, if you now only feel confident with the balance sheet then your next step should be learning about the income statement (the profit & loss statement). The two go hand in hand and when you are confident with both you will find 1 + 1 actually equals 3; the total benefit is greater than the sum of their parts.

There is one more major linkage example that I will discuss, briefly. This is actually something we have already covered, the feeding of earnings (or profit) from the income statement into the equity section of the balance sheet. Simply, last year's retained earnings (last years balance sheet) plus this year's profit (this years income statement) equals this year-end's retained earnings (this year end balance sheet). This is true forever and always, is one of the most understandable linkages and still one of the most important. It also provides a double-checking or feedback mechanism into how stable and accurate all your accounting systems are, remembering that the balance sheet must balance and profit must equal revenue minus expenses. Note: as discussed earlier, dividends affects retained earnings, so technically it is: last year's retained earnings (last years balance sheet) plus this year's profit (this years income statement) *minus dividends paid* equals this year end's retained earnings (this year end's balance sheet).

# Conclusion

Well that's it! I feel great and I hope you feel the same way next time you come across a balance sheet. A famous Columbia University academic once told me that eventually you have to stop learning and start practicing. So while I thank you for wanting to learn about financial statements and purchasing this book, I urge you to take what you know now and start reading over as many balance sheets you can get your hands on. There is always room for more education (and with accounting you can spend a lifetime) but never forget to take the leap and spend more time analyzing your balance sheets. Ask questions of yourself when looking at the accounts and figures: "What is this telling me?" then "and if it says that, what is the next implication? And can I check that with information I already have?" Too often accounting is seen as dry and boring, but accounting is the language of business and business is often our livelihoods; nothing this important should be written-off (an accounting phrase, haha) as dull or someone else's responsibility. Even if you never want to be an accountant, it's great that you are taking the steps so you need not rely on your accountant as heavily, can communicate better with them…and know if they are wasting your money. I hope this is the beginning of a great journey.

Finally, I identify myself as a businessperson as opposed to an author. So I hope, as a businessperson, this book has given you more value than your initial outlay of funds. Thanks for your purchase and your time in reading this book. A picture tells a thousand words: how many words is your balance sheet telling you?

Best wishes!
Axel Tracy

# Extras

## Book Excerpt

As I mentioned at the start of this title, Balance Sheet Basics is part of a series that covers all the three main financial statements. The second book I wrote within this series was *'Income Statement Basics: From Confusion to Comfort in Under 30 Pages'*.

This second book follows a similar format to Balance Sheet Basics and once again looks at the real-world financial statements of Amazon Inc. This time, though, the focus is the Income Statement (also known as the Profit & Loss Statement).

Below you will find an excerpt from this book, so feel free to check it out. If you enjoy the excerpt and want to buy the book, you can find it at Amazon via the link below.

Note: You can also buy the three 'Financial Statement Basics' titles as one, complete book. You can find, "Financial Statement Basics: From Confusion to Comfort in Under 100 Pages" at Amazon and it includes the title you just read as well as "Income Statement Basics" and "Cash Flow Statement Basics".

*Taken from:*

*"Income Statement Basics: From Confusion to Comfort in Under 30 Pages"*
(**http://accofina.com/books/income-statement-basics.html**)

*By Axel Tracy*

# Expenses

*"Expenses are decreases in economic benefits during the accounting period in the form of outflows or depletions of assets or incurrences of liabilities that result in decreases in equity, other than those relating to distributions to equity participants."*

- *IASB Conceptual Framework 4.25(b)*

Above is the definition of expenses according to the IASB and again it has links to the balance sheet even though expenses are within the income statement. The quickest way to make sense of this obtuse definition is to look at the similarities between it and the IASB definition of income in the last section. You will see rather quickly that the two definitions are mirrors of each other and the language is almost identical (it's just mirrored language). From this you can conclude that expenses are the opposite of income and essentially represent the opposite effect within the Income Statement, that being they subtract economic benefits (money) during an accounting period.

If again these definitions are not your preferred method of learning, the simplest way to look at it is that expenses are the ongoing costs to run the business during a set accounting period. They are things like office rents and marketing expenses. The things you need to pay for in the ordinary course of business. Using a basic definition again and mirroring the earlier statement, we can say that the 'basic' concept is: *Expenses are the monies you spend or incur while in the ordinary course of selling goods or selling services (keeping in mind the accrual accounting concept).*

Expenses take up most of the remaining Income Statement aside from the calculation results. That is, they lie beneath the income section and roll all the way down to the net income figure (aside from calculation results along the way).

Looking at a real-world example you can see Amazon's expenses (within the included Income Statement) include operating expenses, non-operating expenses and tax expenses (tax provisions to be specific).

Before we go any further, it is time to talk about a number of different formatting options to describe how the expenses are set out in the income statement.

*Alternative 1a 'Descriptive Format':*

This alternative is just the option that Amazon.com has taken in our example. The descriptive format displays the revenue figure and simply subtracts all expenses to leave a net income figure.

You can see with Amazon.com that they have set out their Income Statement with an 'operating expenses' section that provides most of the detail of their day-to-day operations, which is directly below the revenue figures. Amazon divides their ordinary expenses into certain categories (such as Cost of Sales & Fulfilment) and simply allocates all ordinary expenses into one of these categories.

*Note:* It is often important to read the Notes to the Financial

Statements (the 'fine print') to get further clarification into the brief (1-page) set of results are calculated and allocated. After doing this with Amazon, I found out that they even break down their depreciation expenses into their respective operating expense categories, such as some depreciation for 'Fulfilment' and some depreciation for 'Technology & content'. Many businesses separate out depreciation and amortization and it was only through reading the fine print (the 'Notes') that I learned that they used this particular accounting policy. Different accounting policies can have very wide implications for financial statement analysis, so the more comfortable you are with getting your head around the basics, the more you should delve into the financial statement Notes to get even more detail.

Okay, getting back to topic, in short: the descriptive format shows revenue minus expenses equals net income.

*Alternative 1b 'Functional Format':*

The next common format is the functional format income statement. While essentially displaying the same information (all income statements essentially show the same thing), the functional format inserts a 'gross profit' section just below the revenue section. That is, revenue minus 'cost of sales' equals gross profit, and only then the rest of the expenses are listed. The functional format separates out cost of sales and gross profit from all the other expenses. This format is common in retailing and manufacturing business (as 'cost of sales' play a large influence) while the descriptive format is more common in service businesses (as 'cost of sales' play a smaller role).

Here is a quick aside if you are unsure as to what 'cost of sales' are: Cost of sales, a.k.a. Cost of Goods Sold (COGS) or Cost of Revenue, are those expenses/costs which are incurred to get inventory that will later be resold. Perhaps in a retailing business cost of sales are the prices paid to wholesalers for the goods the retailer sells. Or perhaps in a manufacturing business, cost of sales are the costs/expenses incurred in manufacturing products that will later be resold.

Do you see why cost of sales and gross profit figures are vital indicators (and hence the functional format) for businesses that hold inventory? Costs of Sales are unavoidable (and often large) expenses for some businesses so their measurement and ongoing management are very important. And gross profit figures (Revenue minus Cost of Sales equals Gross Profit) are also very important as they represent the starting point to meet all other expenses and net income.

Below the gross profit section, the descriptive format and functional format are the same. It is only the inserted gross profit section that makes the income statement a functional format statement.

*'accofina' is the business behind this book and within its website, accofina.com, you will find a number of free resources available for download or for use on-site:*

## Free accofina.com Books

*Accounting Introduction PDF mini-book* **(http://accofina.com/free-books/accounting-foundations.html )** *"Accounting: Foundation Inputs & Outputs"* is a 15-page PDF mini-book which is available for download. It offers some of the basic accounting theory into the inputs and outputs of a financial accounting system. The outputs being the three main financial statements and the inputs being the theory behind accounting data entry.

*331 Great Quotes for Entrepreneurs* **(http://accofina.com/free-books/331-great-quotes-entrepreneurs.html)** This titles offers a broad range of historic and memorable quotes aimed at uplifting and inspiring entrepreneurs with their journey. The book is broken down into 12 major categories, or skills, that should hopefully lead any entrepreneur to success.

## Free accofina.com Spreadsheets

*Ratio Analysis Spreadsheet* **(http://accofina.com/spreadsheets/ratio-analysis-excel.html)** 17 popular financial ratios have been put into a MS Excel Spreadsheet which both calculates the ratios as well as offering the formulae behind them. This spreadsheet comes as a download with three other free accounting and finance spreadsheets.

*Capital Budgeting Spreadsheet*
**(http://accofina.com/spreadsheets/capital-budgeting-excel.html)** If you wish to assess the value of planned large projects and capital expenditures then you may benefit from capital budgeting tools. You can access a spreadsheet that does a lot of number crunching and provides NPVs, pro forma income statements as well as other information just by inputting some key project data.

*Time Value of Money Spreadsheet*
**(http://accofina.com/spreadsheets/time-value-money-excel.html)** The Time Value of Money is one of the most important concepts in finance. This available spreadsheet calculates some of the primary time value of money concepts such as future values, present values and annuities. All formulae are also provided within.

*Retirement Planner Spreadsheet*
**(http://accofina.com/spreadsheets/retirement-planner-excel.html)** With this spreadsheet you can test out a variety of retirement scenarios which will allow you to assess how much savings you need to put in your retirement account during your working life dependent on your expected level of expenditure during retirement.

*Cash Flow Forecast Spreadsheet*
**(http://accofina.com/cash-flow-forecast-excel.html)** The final spreadsheet offered by accofina is a 2-year monthly cash flow forecast to assist in planning and control. It provides a strong overview of 24-months and also calculates running balances, aggregate totals and overdraft interest.

# More Books and Other accofina Products

**More Books:**

1) Ratio Analysis Fundamentals
http://accofina.com/books/ratio-analysis-fundamentals.html

2) Income Statement Basics (Book 2)
http://accofina.com/books/income-statement-basics.html

3) Cash Flow Statement Basics (Book 3)
http://accofina.com/books/cash-flow-statement-basics.html

4) Financial Statement Basics (Balance Sheet Basics plus Books 2 & 3)
http://accofina.com/books/financial-statement-basics.html

5) Corporate Finance Fundamentals
http://accofina.com/books/corporate-finance-fundamentals.html

**iOS Apps:**

1) Ratio Analysis & Management Accounting Calculators
http://accofina.com/apps/management-accounting-ratio-analysis-app.html

2) Profitable Pricing
http://accofina.com/apps/profitable-pricing-app.html

**Online Courses and Tutorials:**

1) Financial Statement Fundamentals (Udemy)
**http://accofina.com/online-education/financial-statement-fundamentals.html**

2) Udemy Instructor Page
**www.udemy.com/u/axeltracy/**

3) YouTube Channel
**www.youtube.com/accofina**

# Author Contact Details and Review Requests

You can contact me anytime and for any reason at any of these contact points. Tell me if you enjoyed the book, or if you could suggest anything for a 2nd edition.

Email: **axel@accofina.com**
Facebook: **facebook.com/accofinaDotCom**
Twitter: **@accofina**
Google+: **https://plus.google.com/+accofina**

**Amazon Review Request:**
Also, I'd love to get an Amazon Review from you if you enjoyed, and got value, from this book.

Positive Amazon Reviews are worth their weight gold in the Amazon World and could possibly propel my little business beyond my wildest expectations. If you did get a positive experience from this book, I'd deeply appreciate it if you could spare a couple of minutes to Rate the book on the Amazon product page and maybe leave a positive Comment. Thanks again.

**GoodReads Review Request:**
I'm hoping to become a more active author on GoodReads. I'm still learning myself, but it looks like a pretty cool reading, writing and sharing platform. If you received value from this book and you're happy to leave a review, but would prefer GoodReads over Amazon, then you should find all my books on GoodReads too.

Here is my author page:
https://www.goodreads.com/author/show/7450542.Axel_Tracy

Printed in Great Britain
by Amazon